Europe Cities Sketch Vol.3
Adult Coloring Book

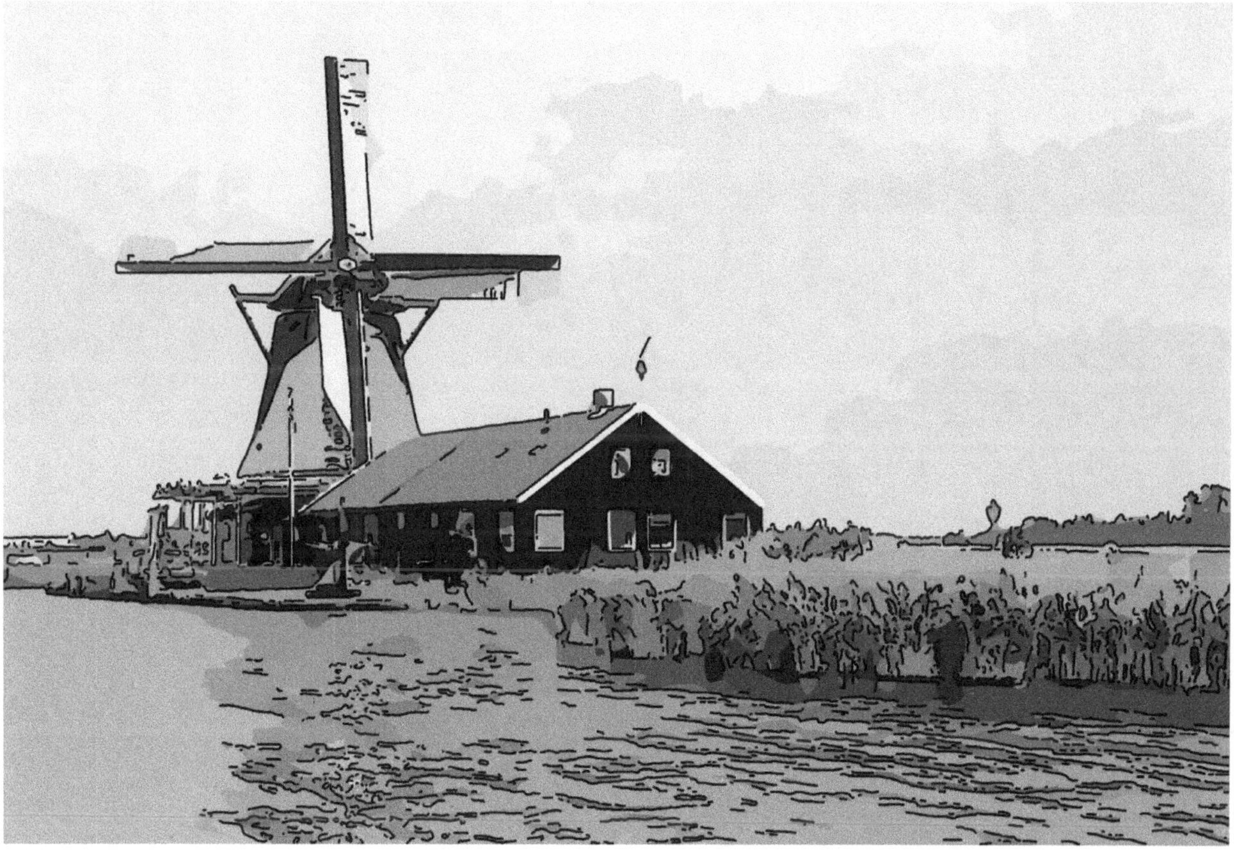

Annie Jr.

Europe Cities Sketch Vol.3
Adult Coloring Book

ISBN-13: 978-1537715698

ISBN-10: 1537715690

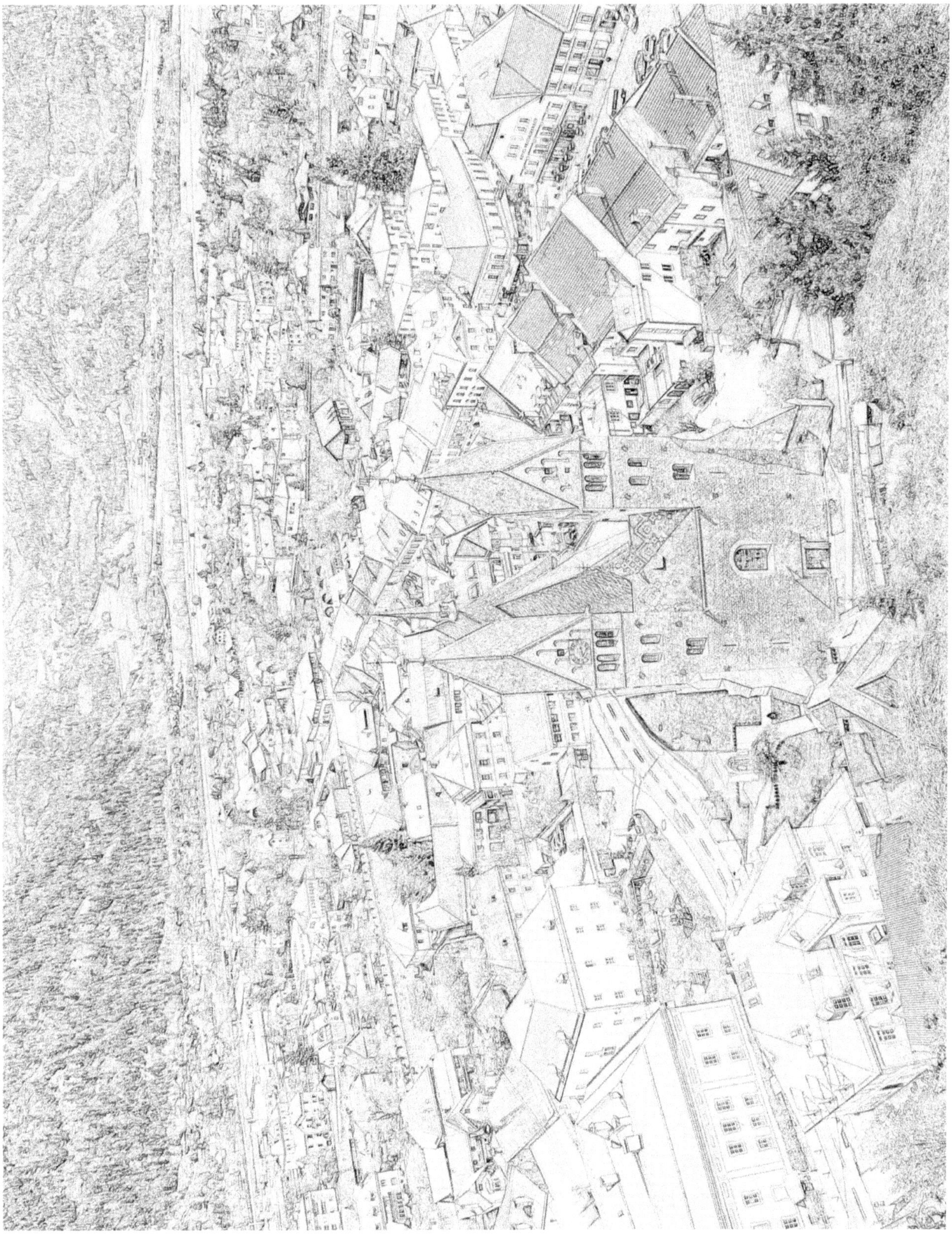

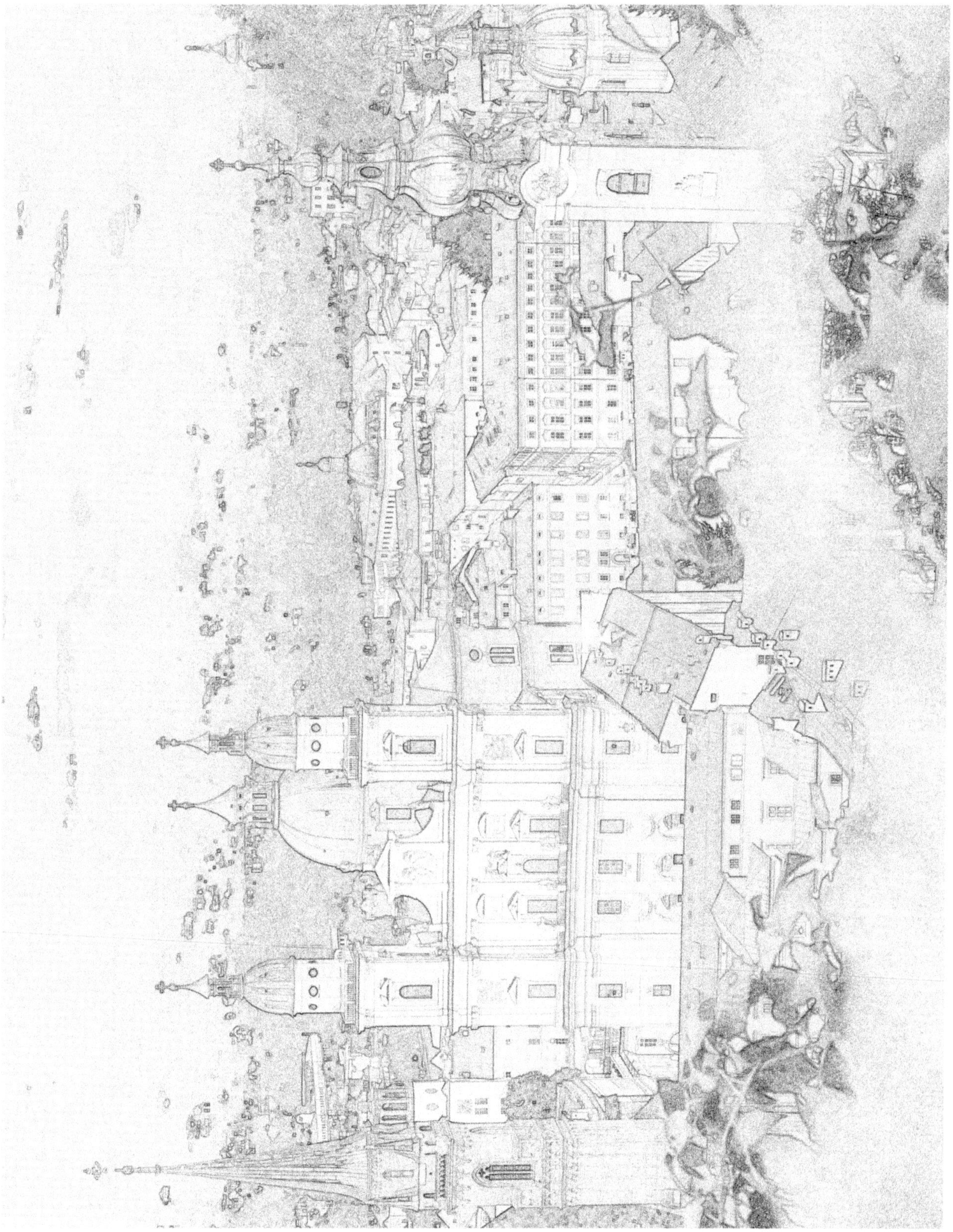

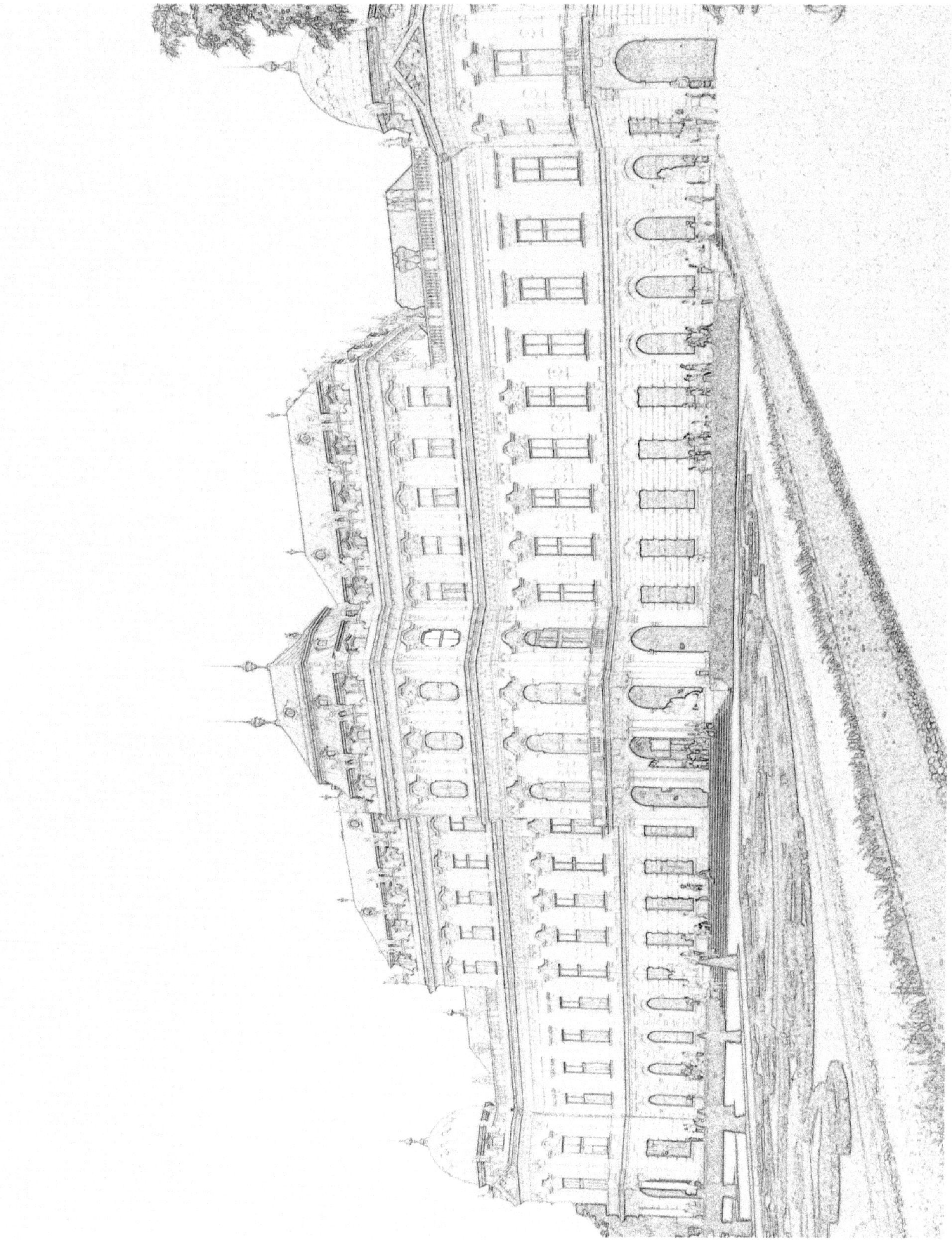

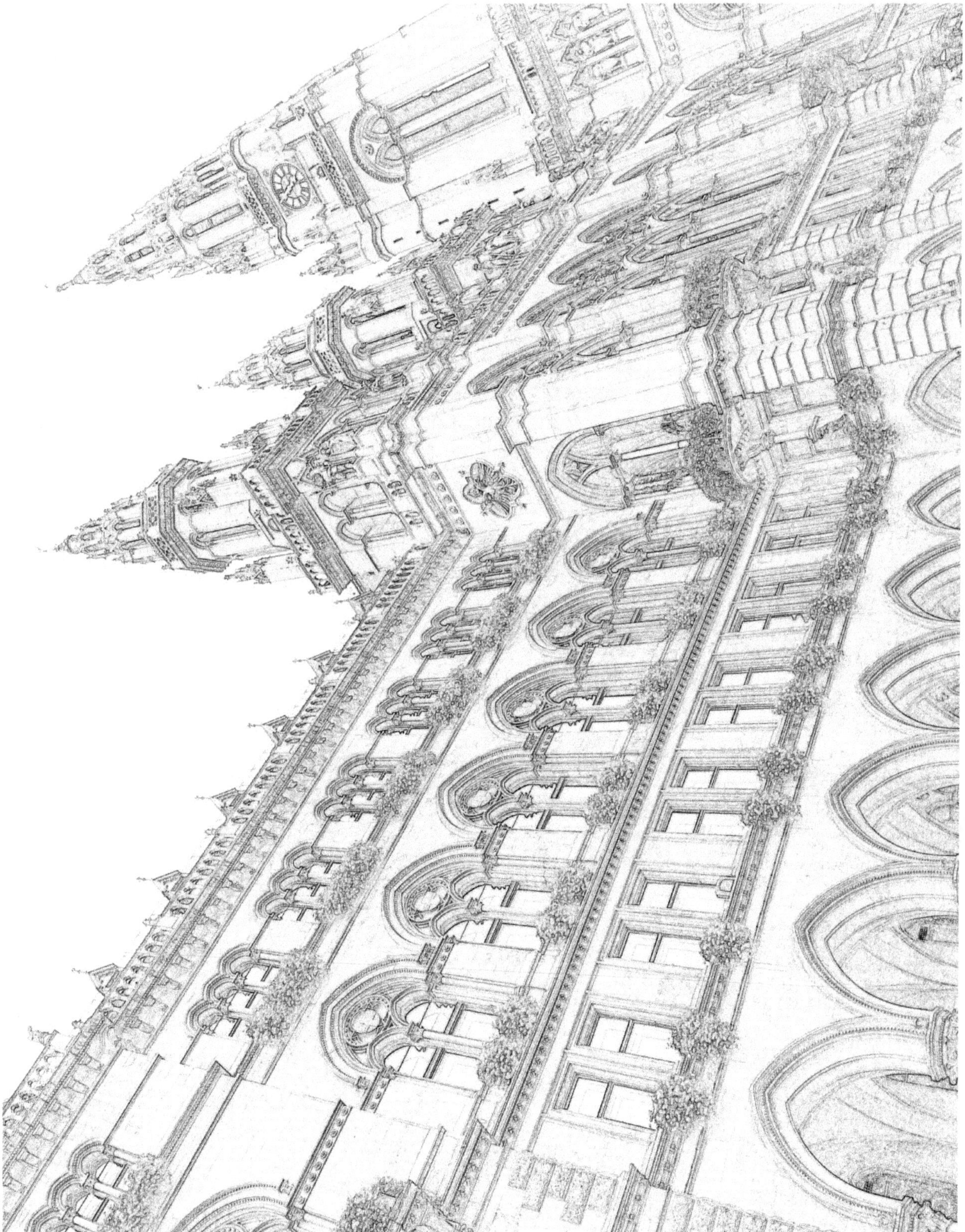

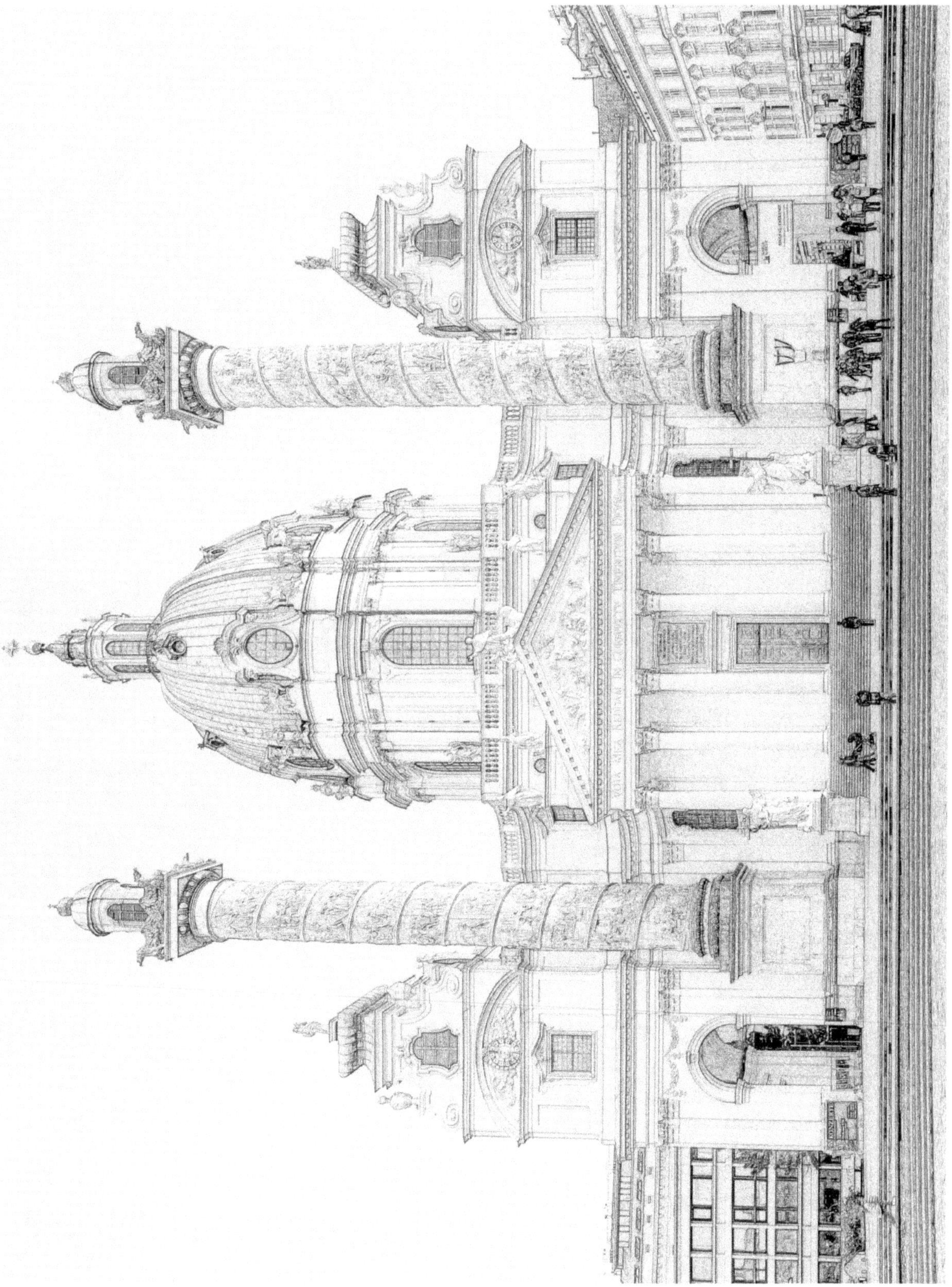

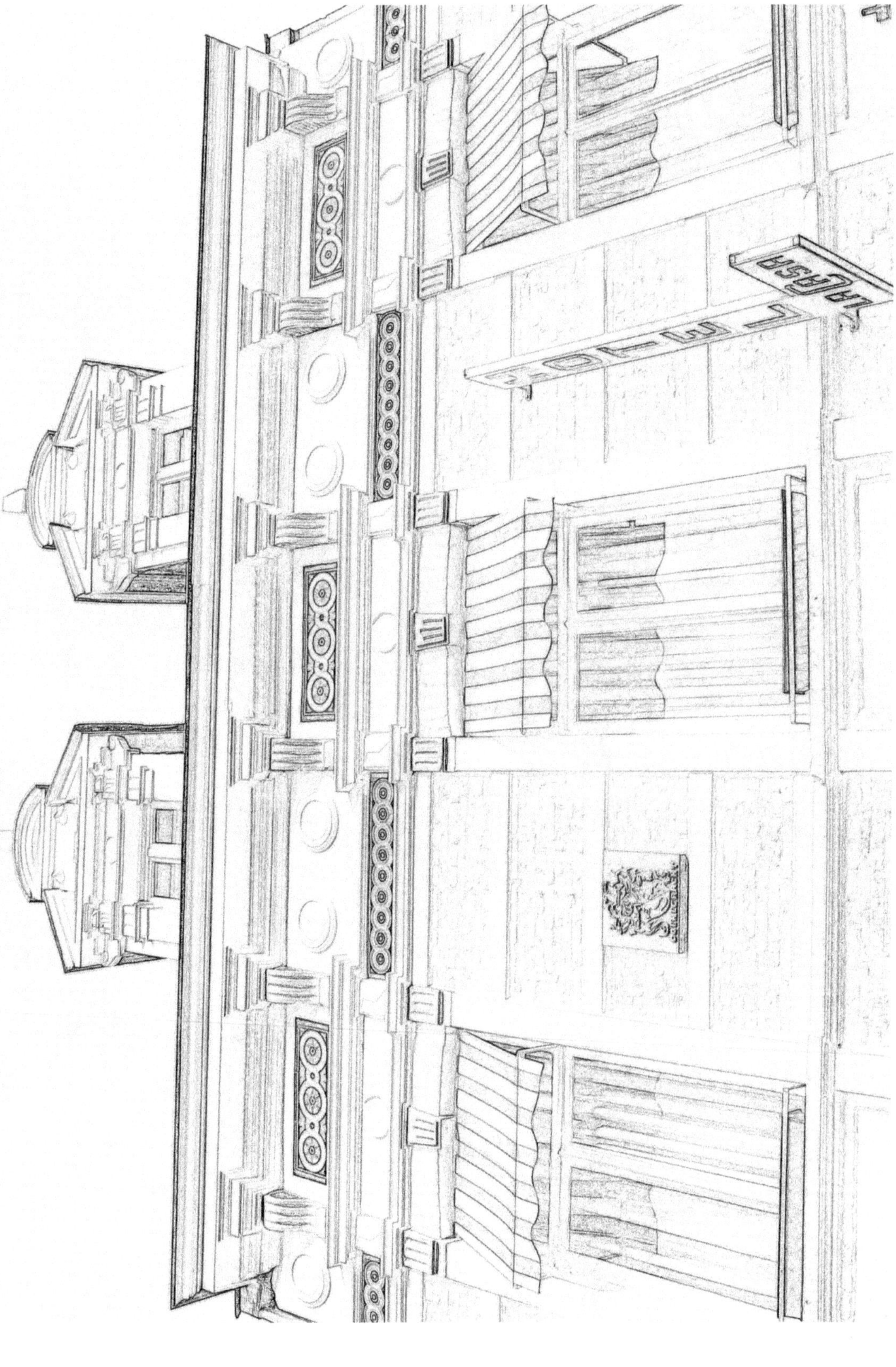

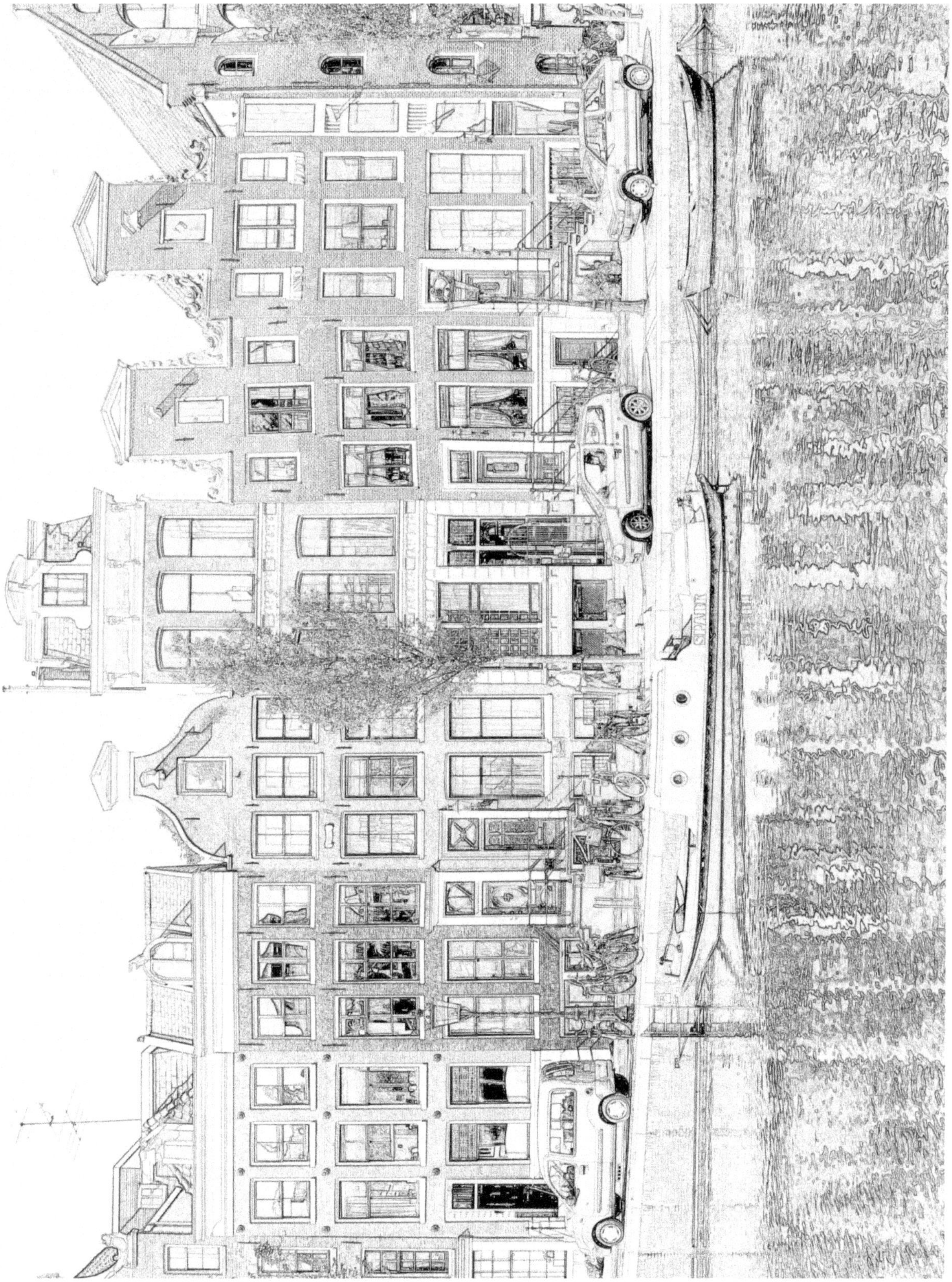

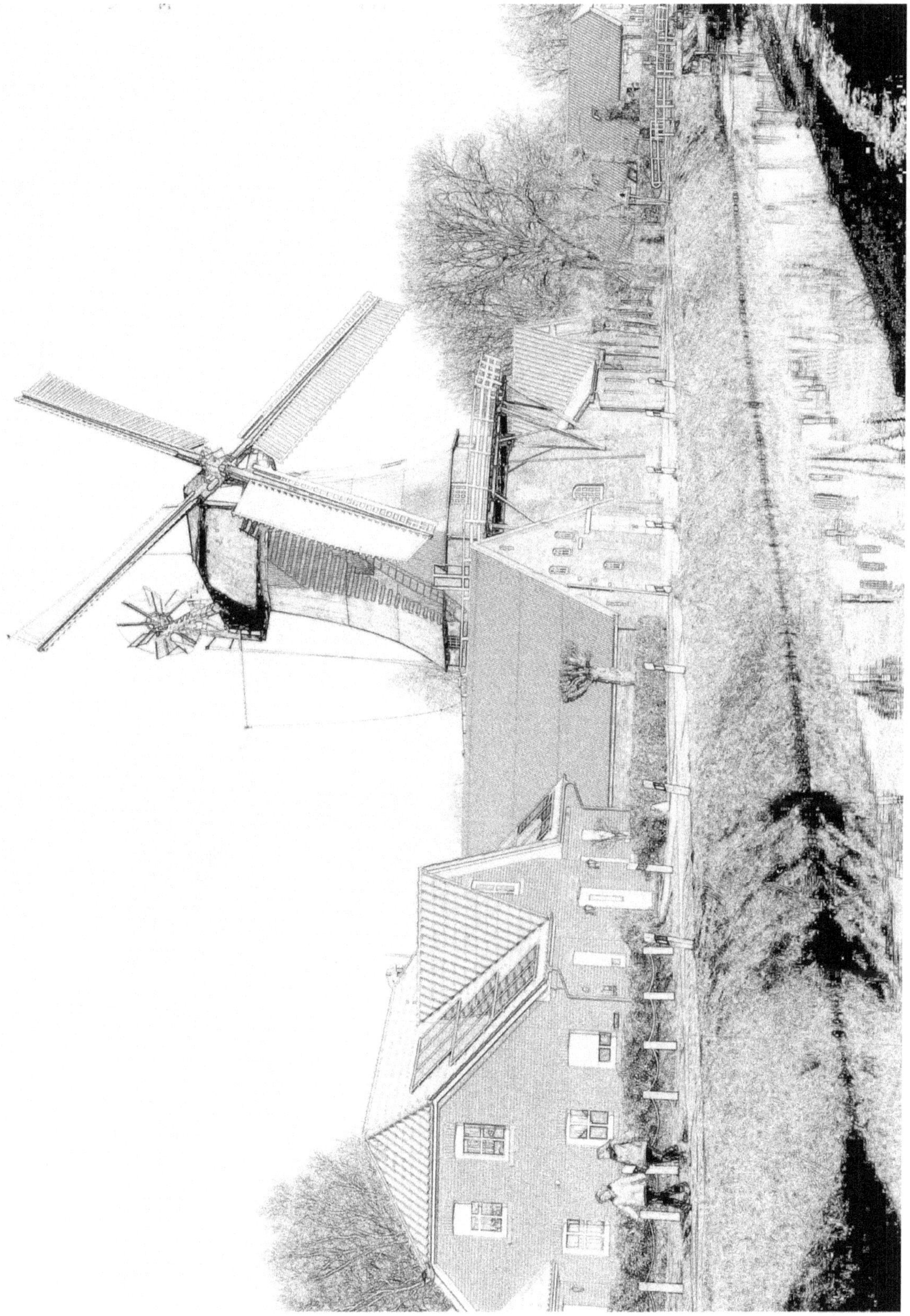

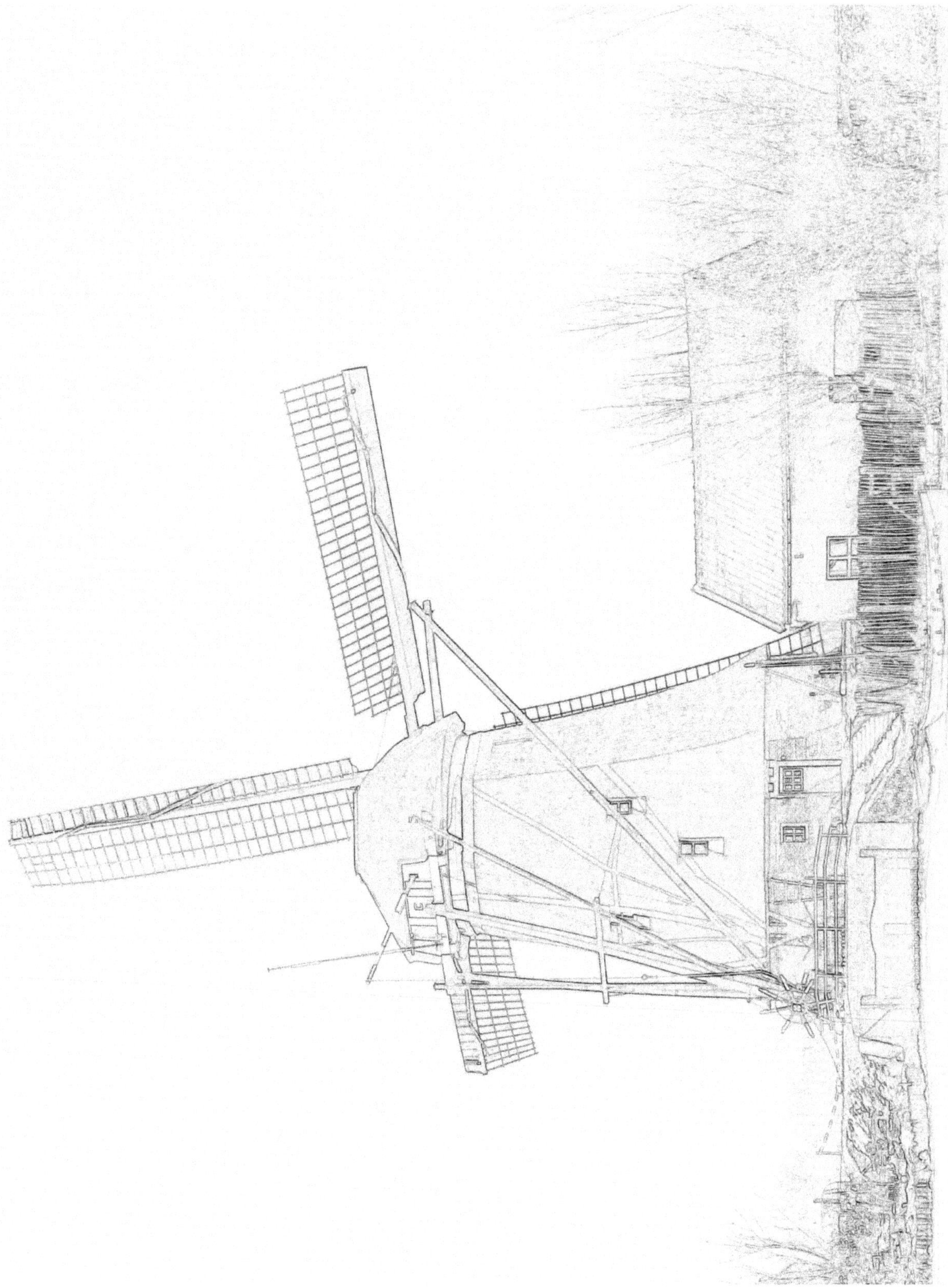

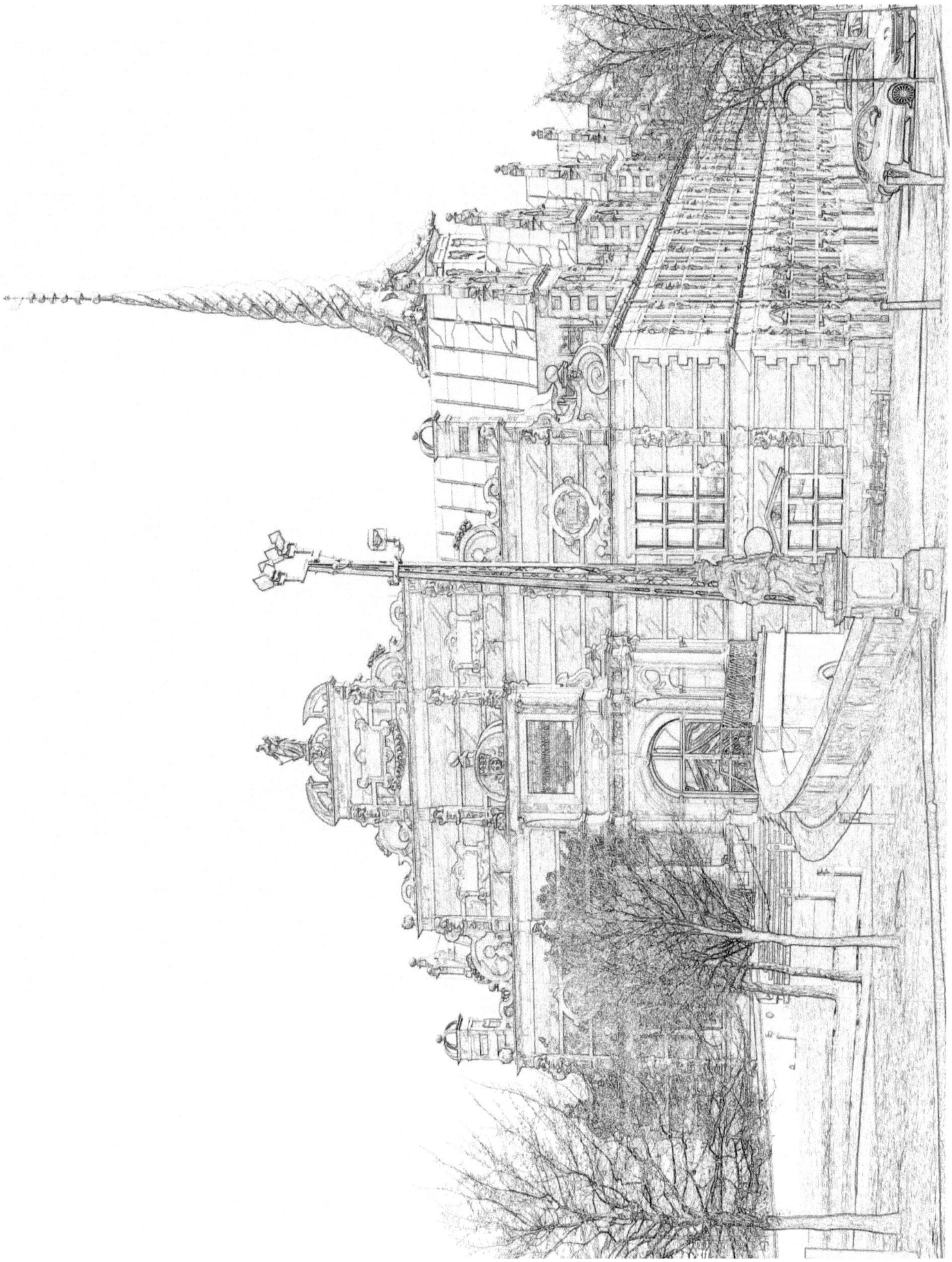

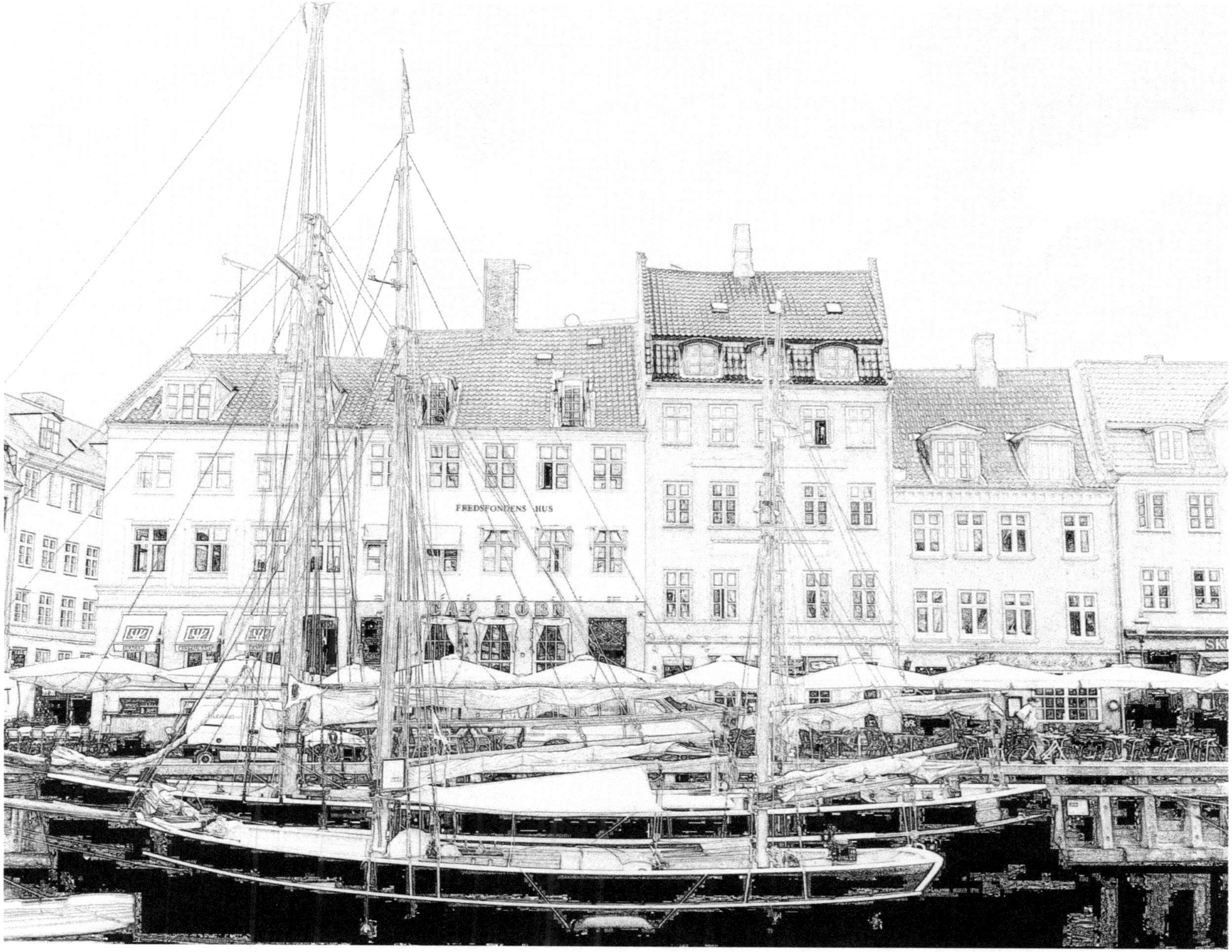
FREDSFONDENS HUS
CAP HORN

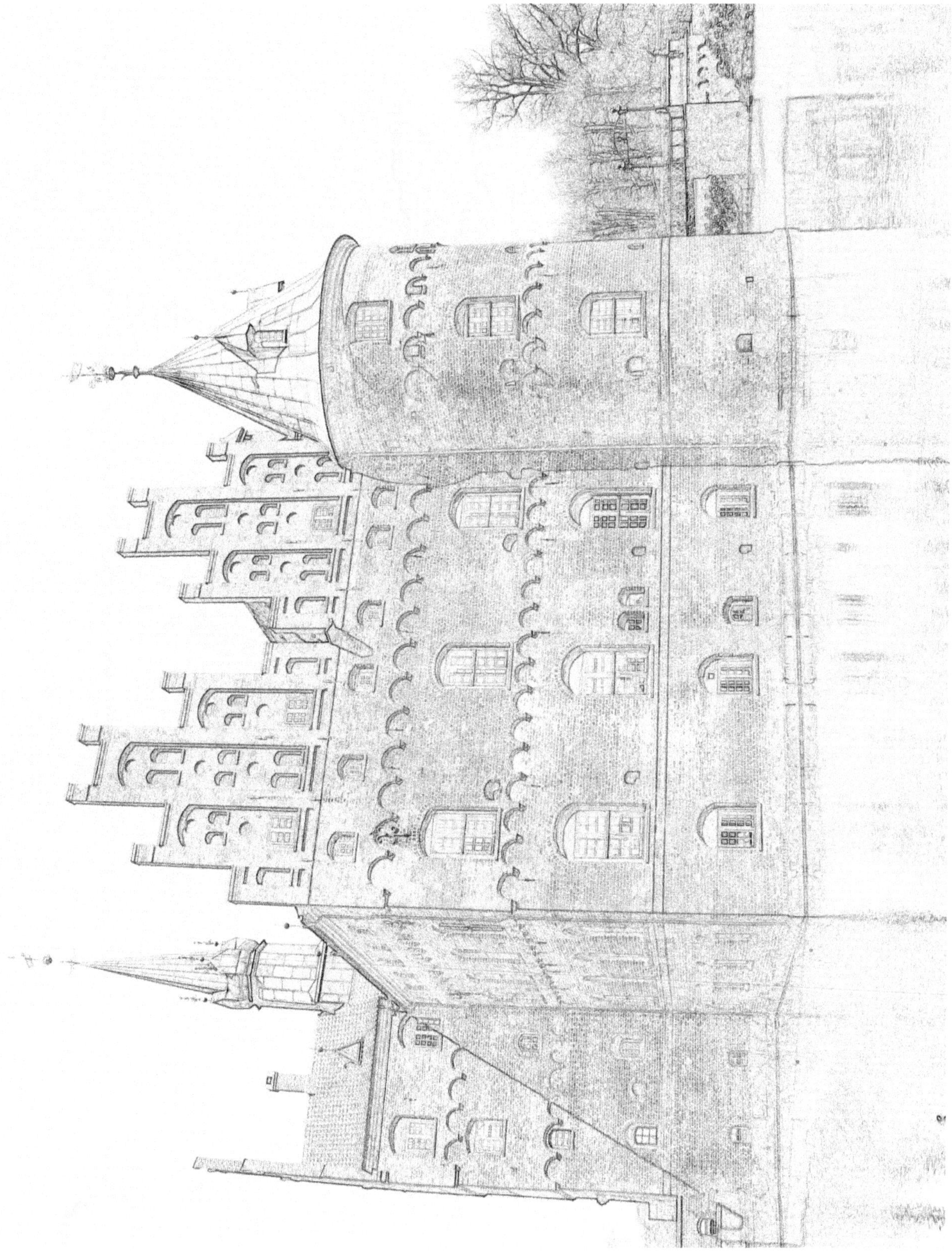

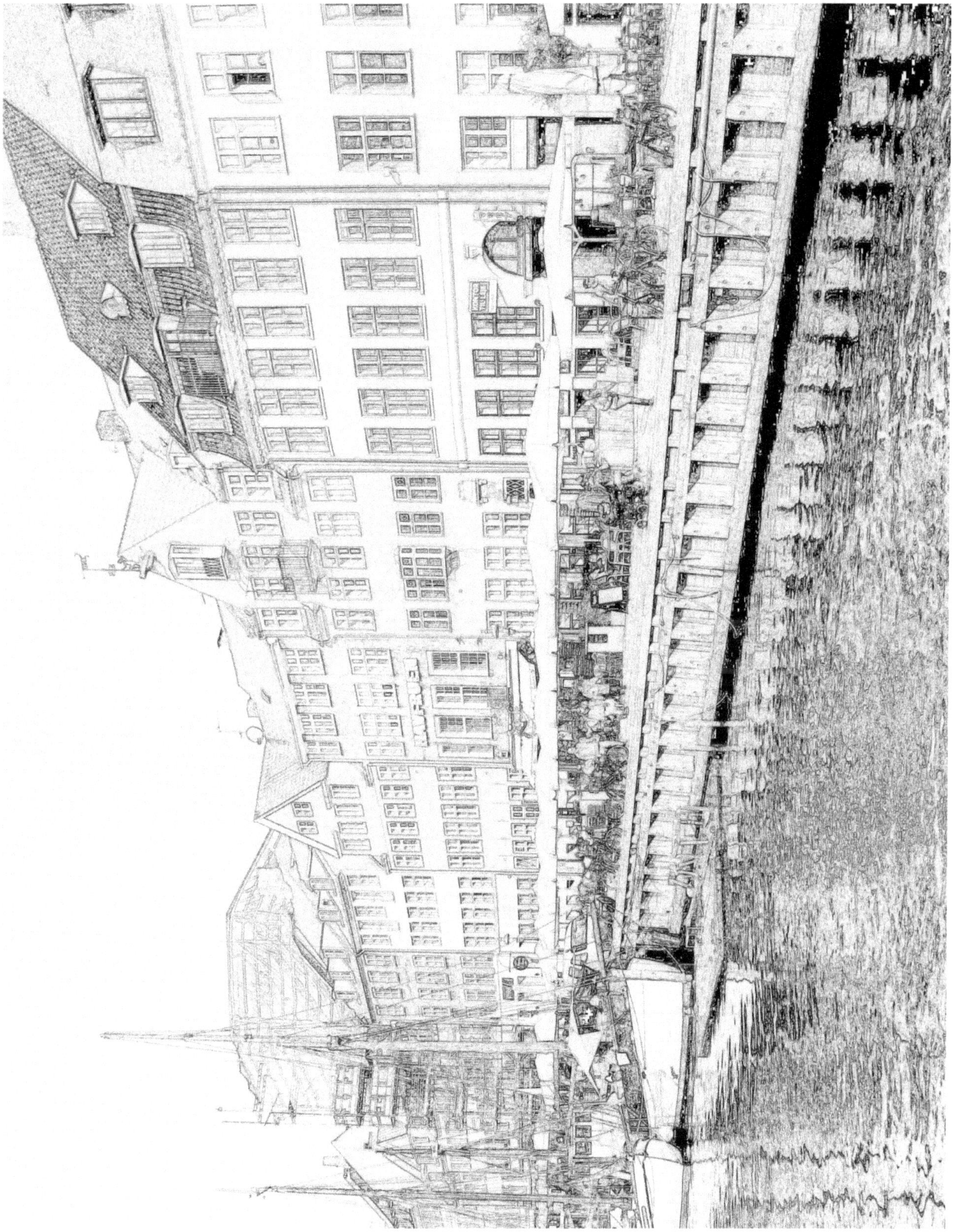

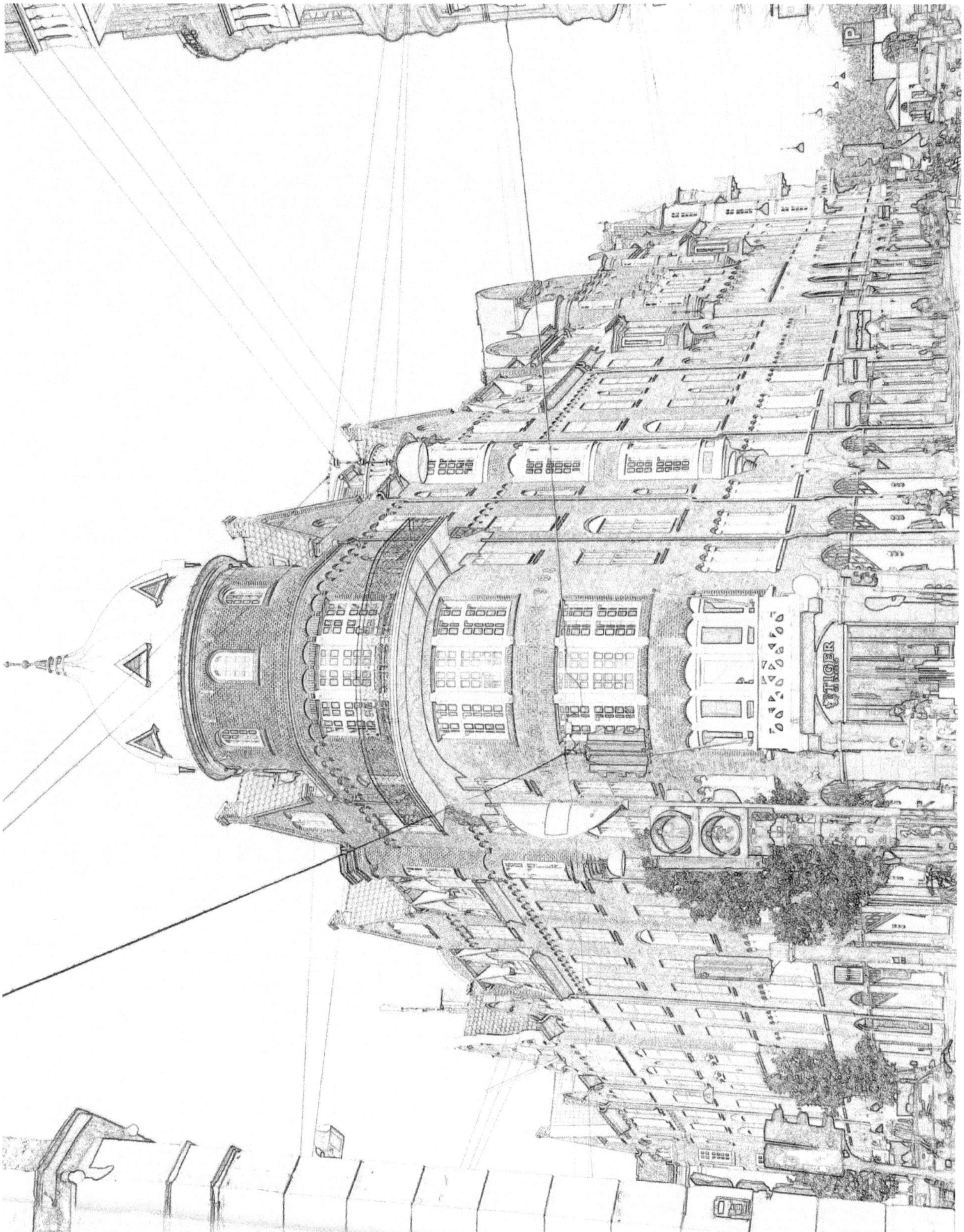
TIGER

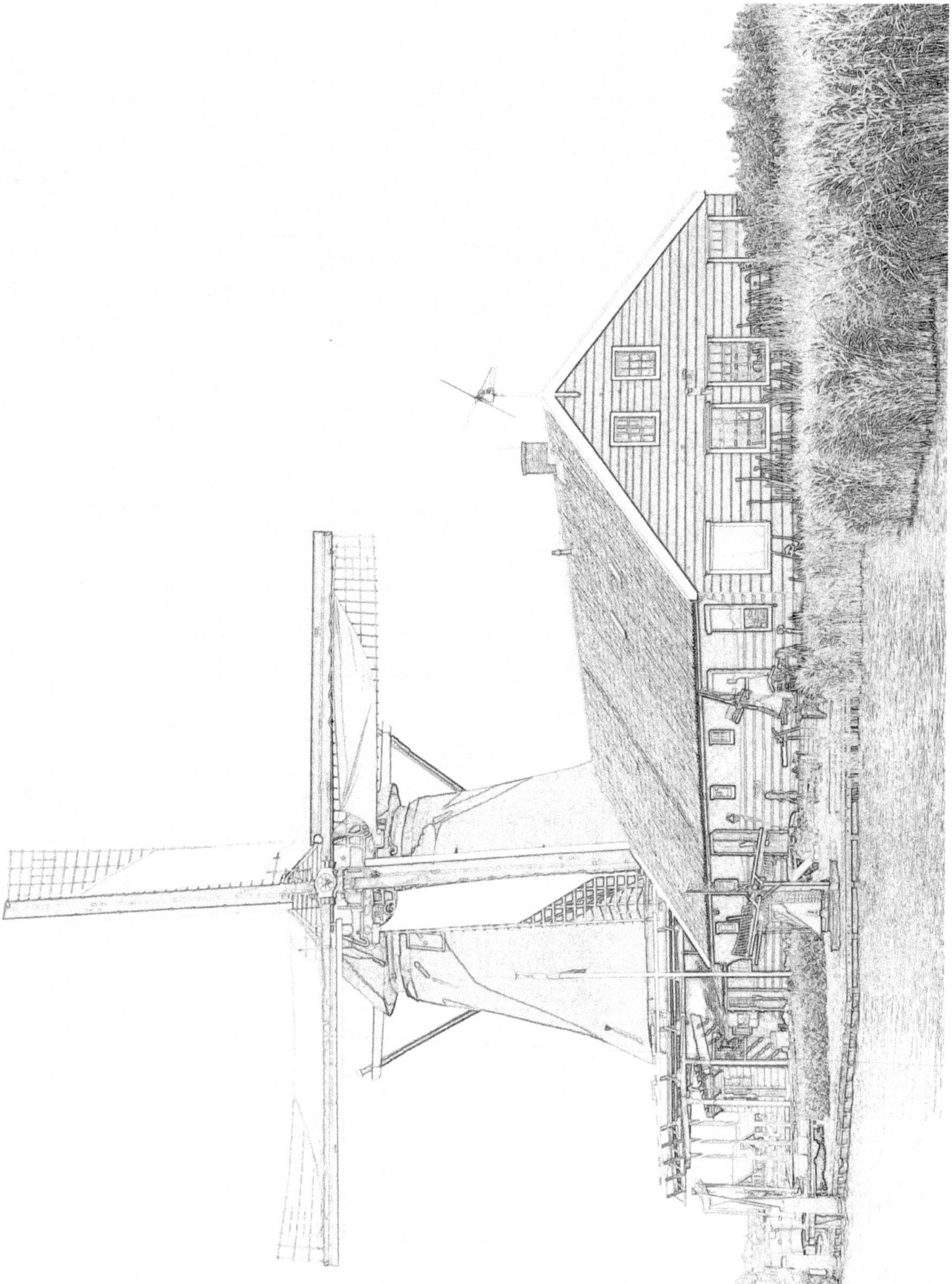

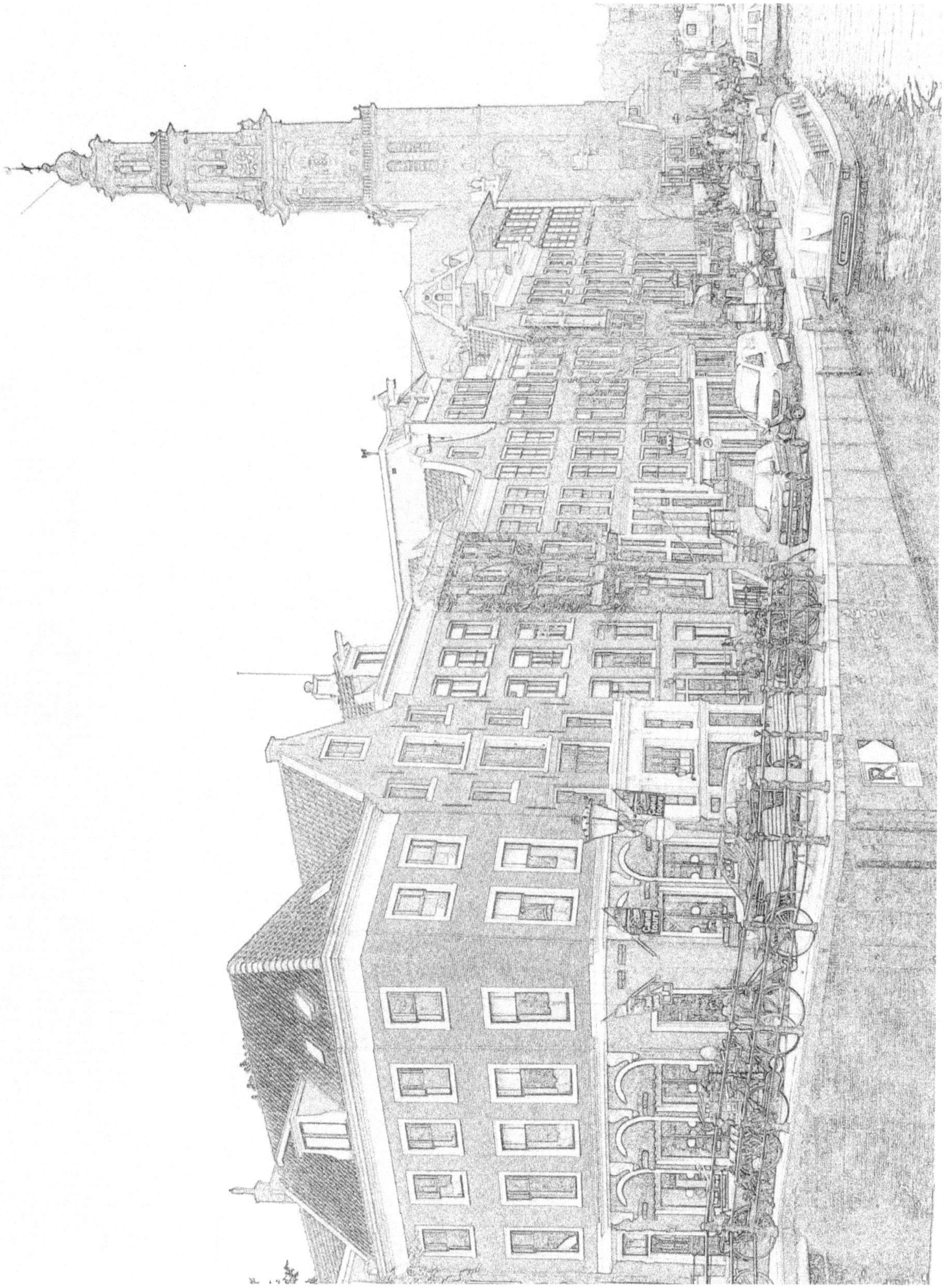

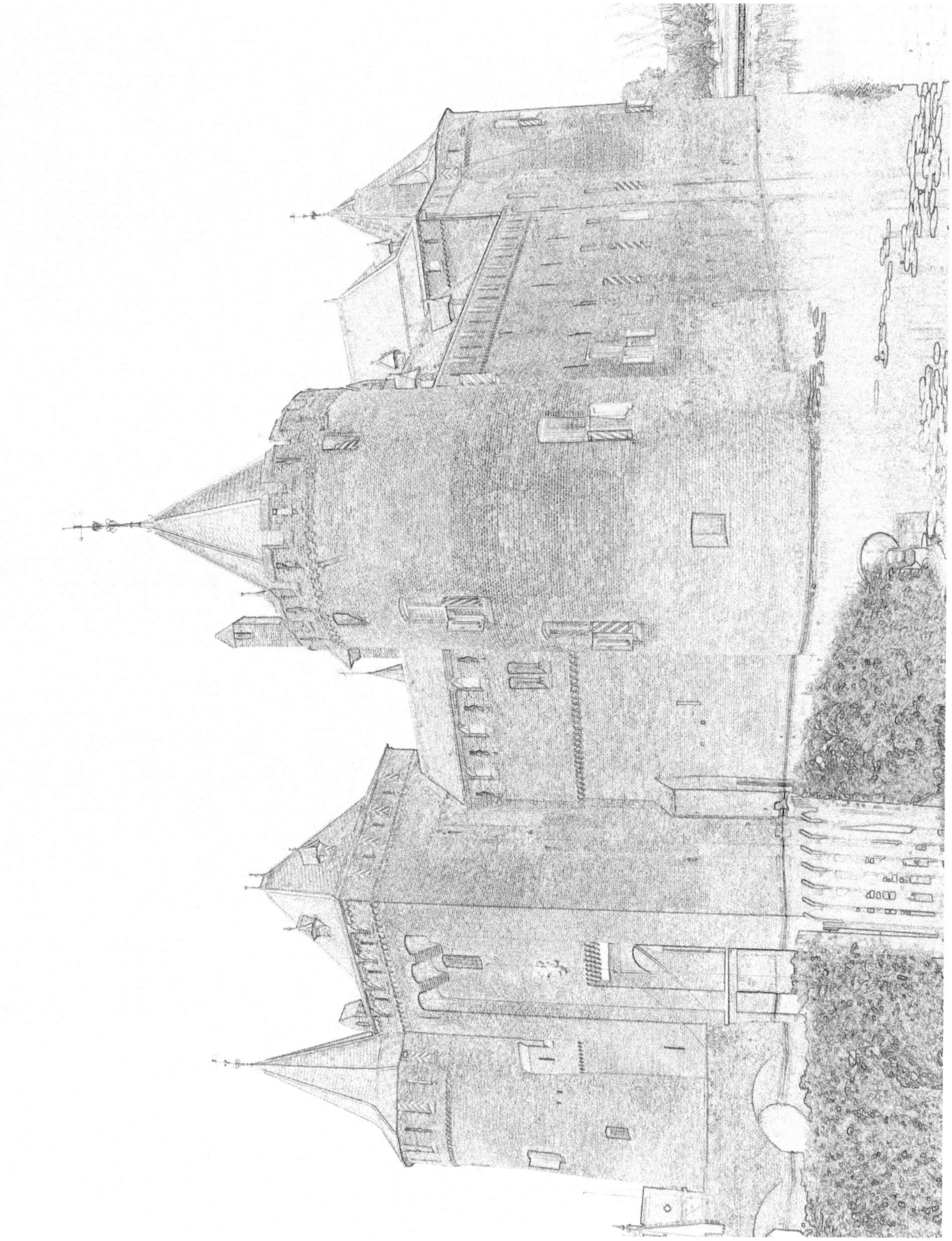

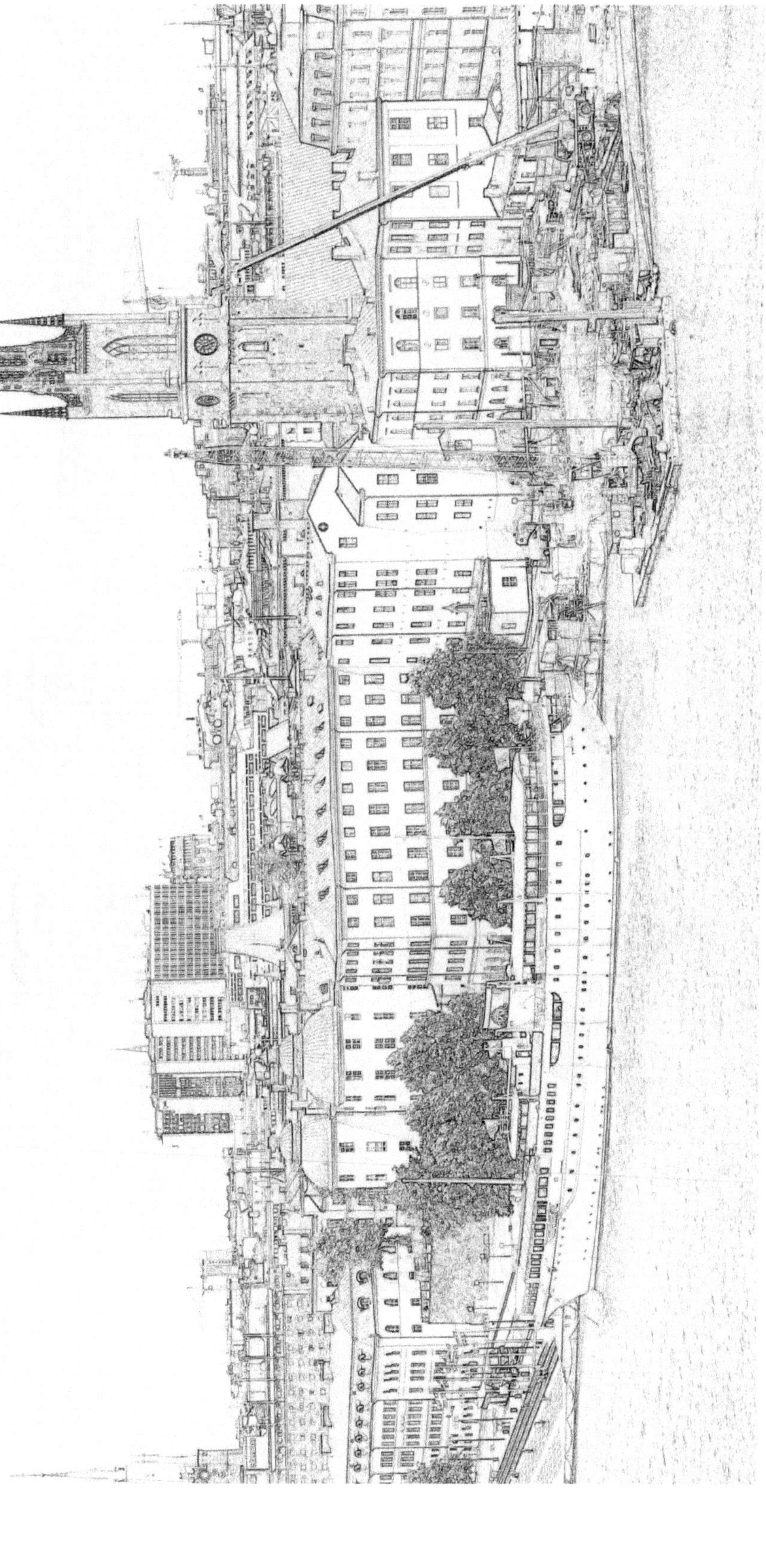

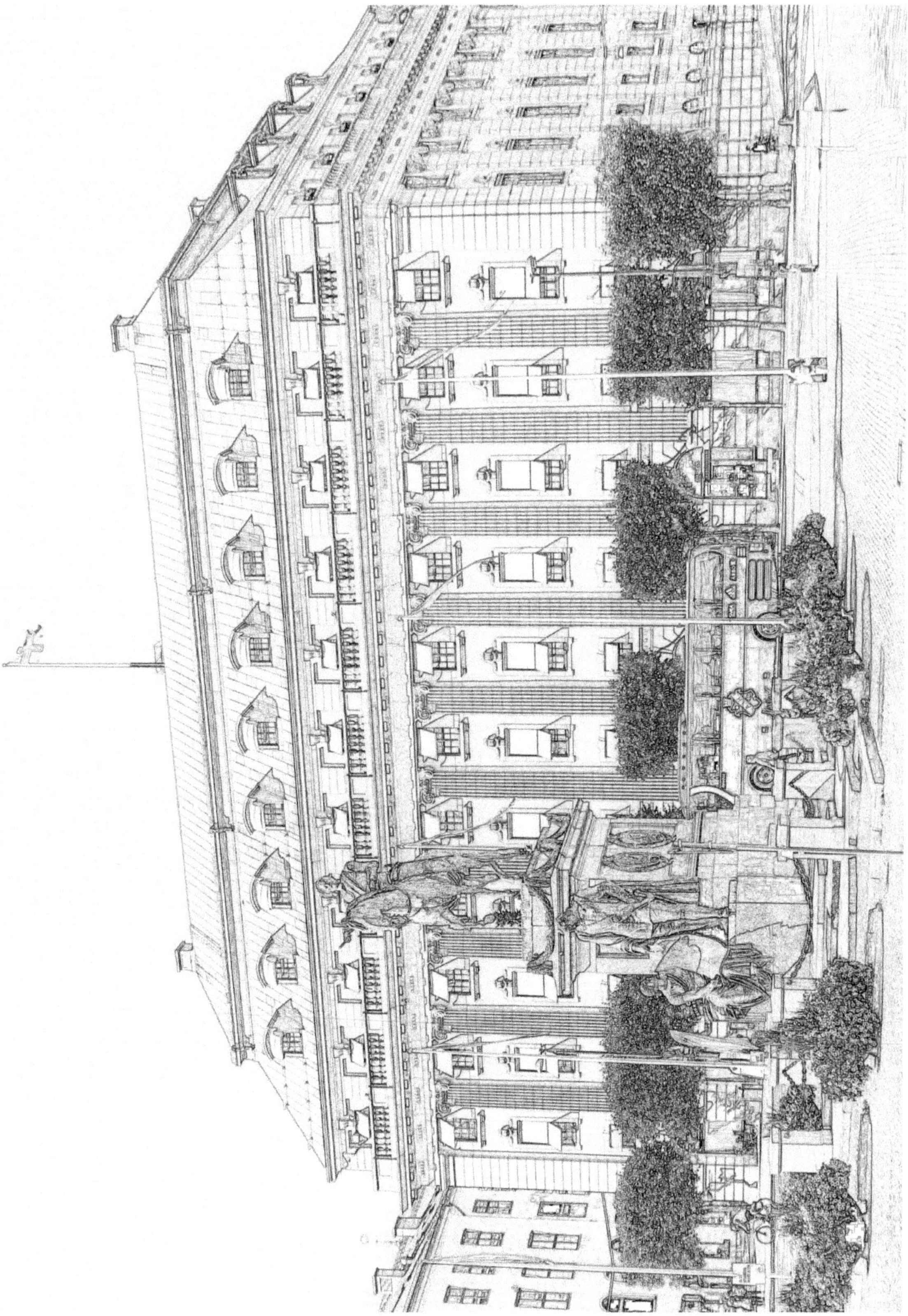

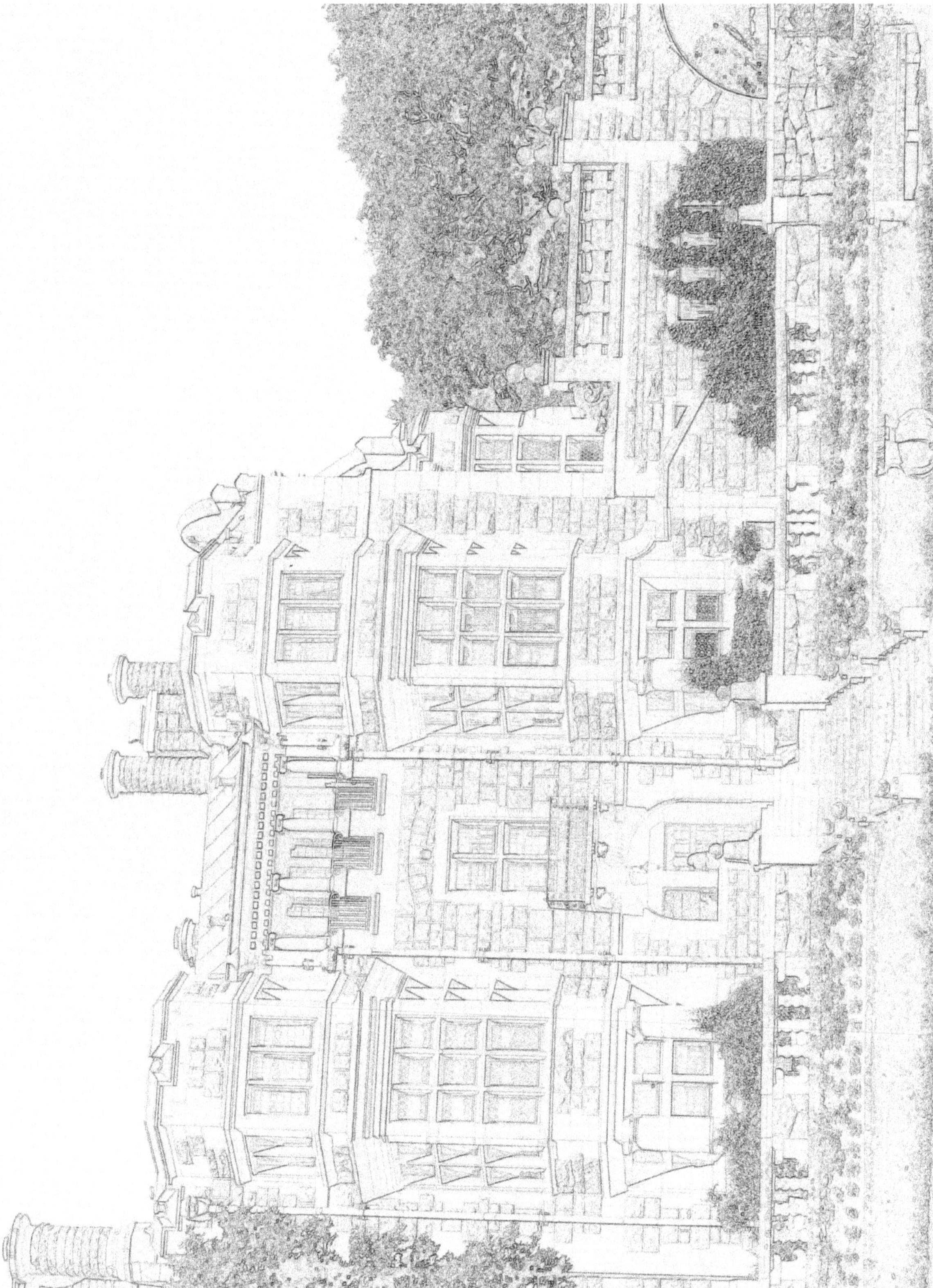

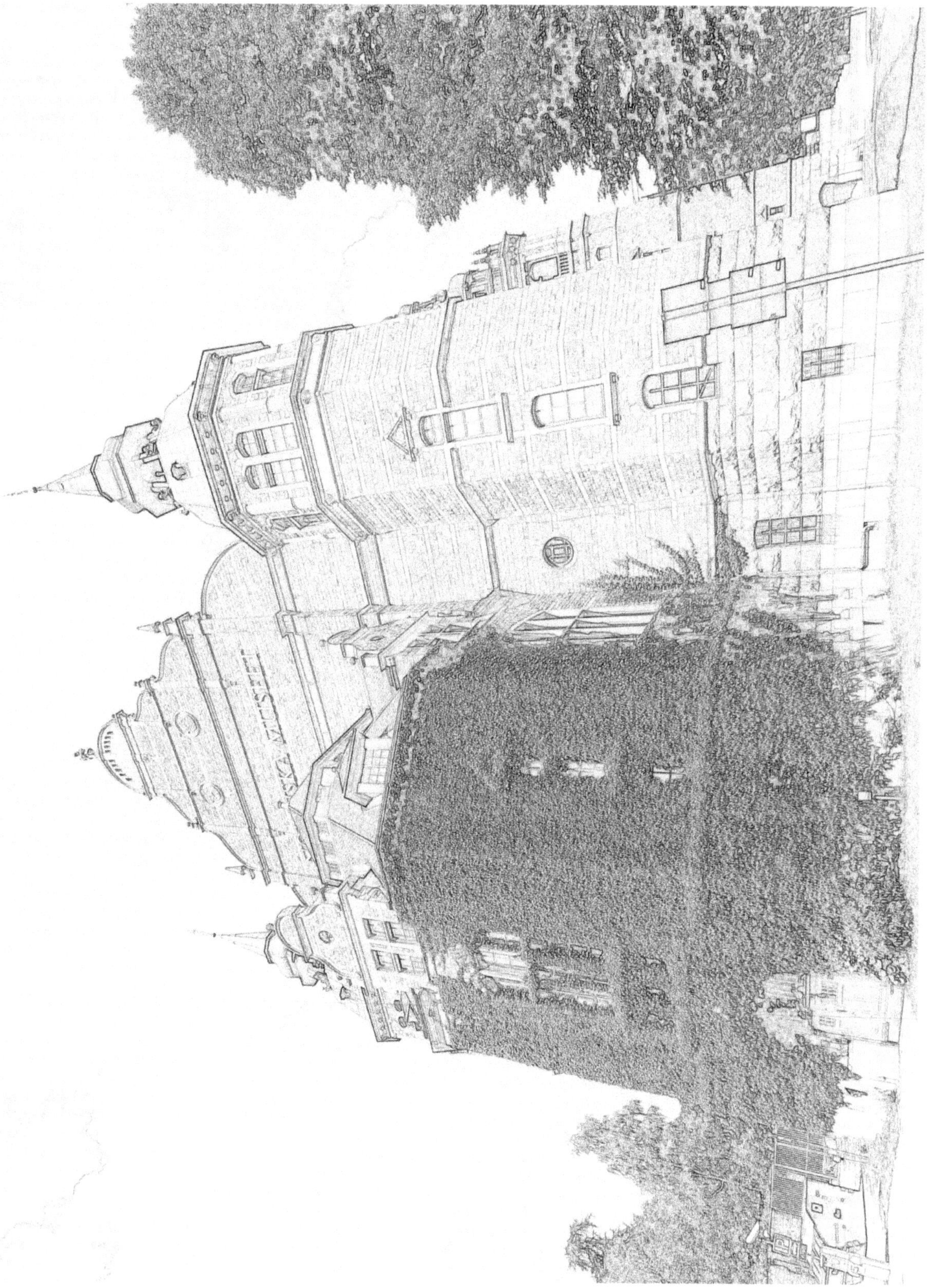

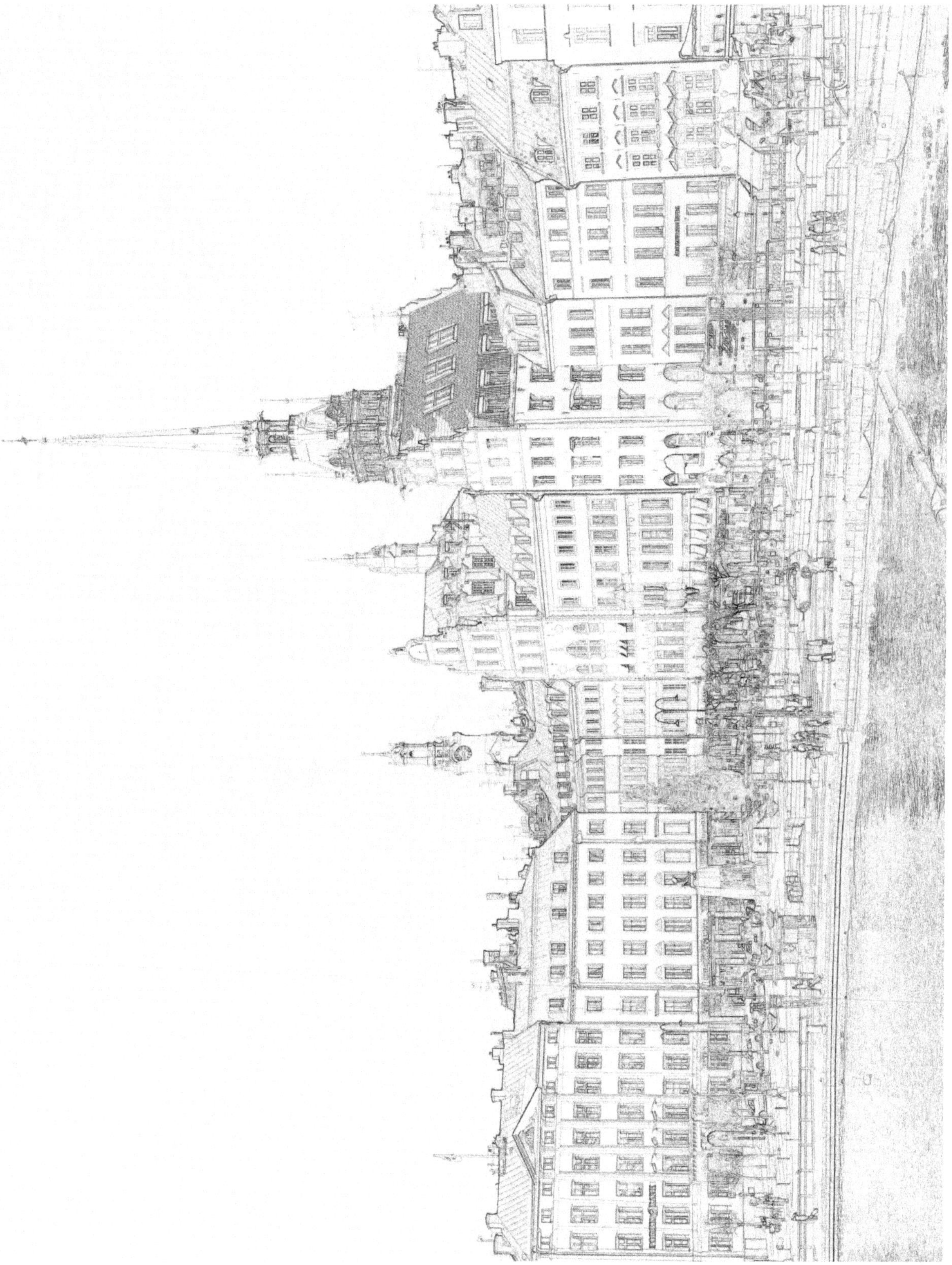

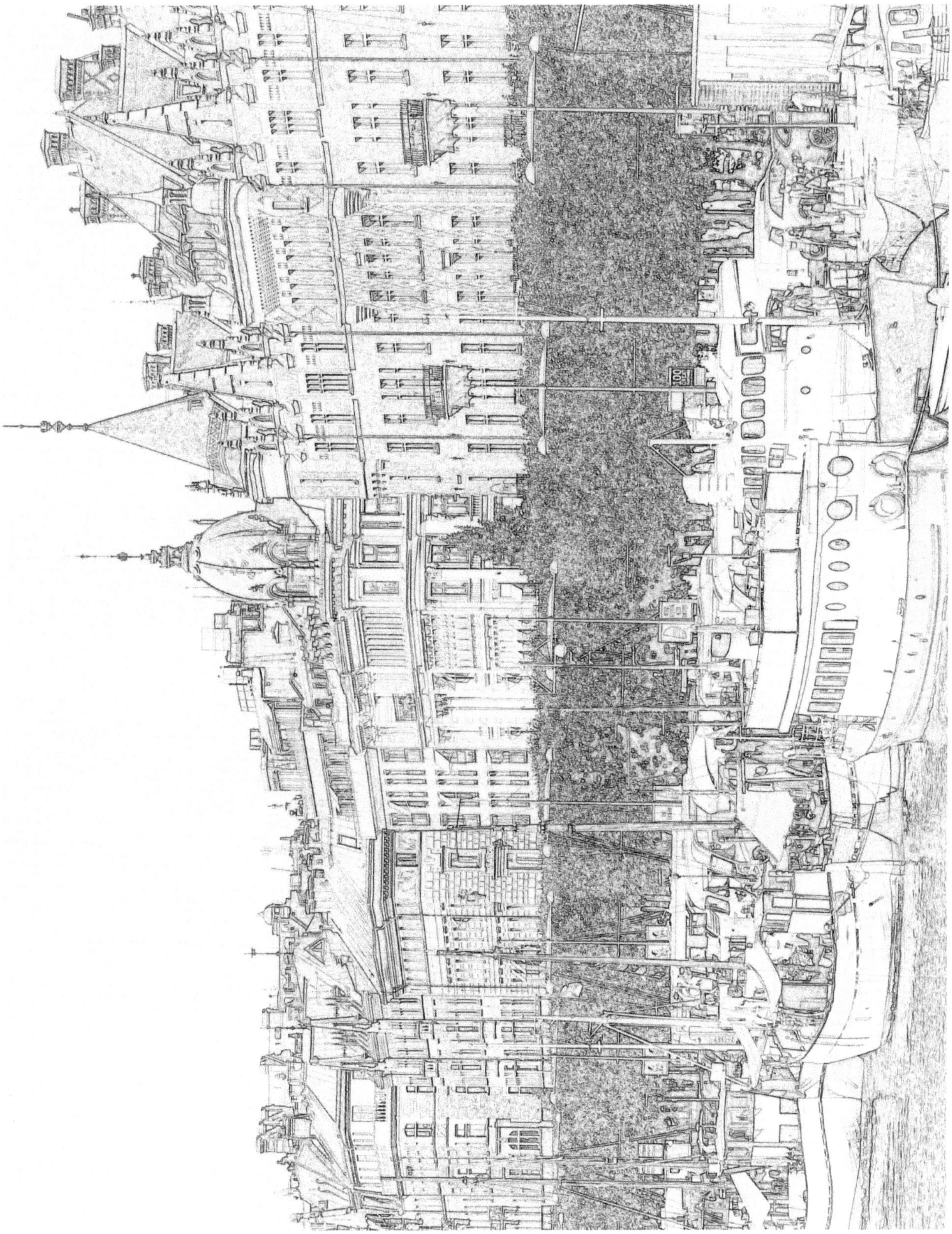

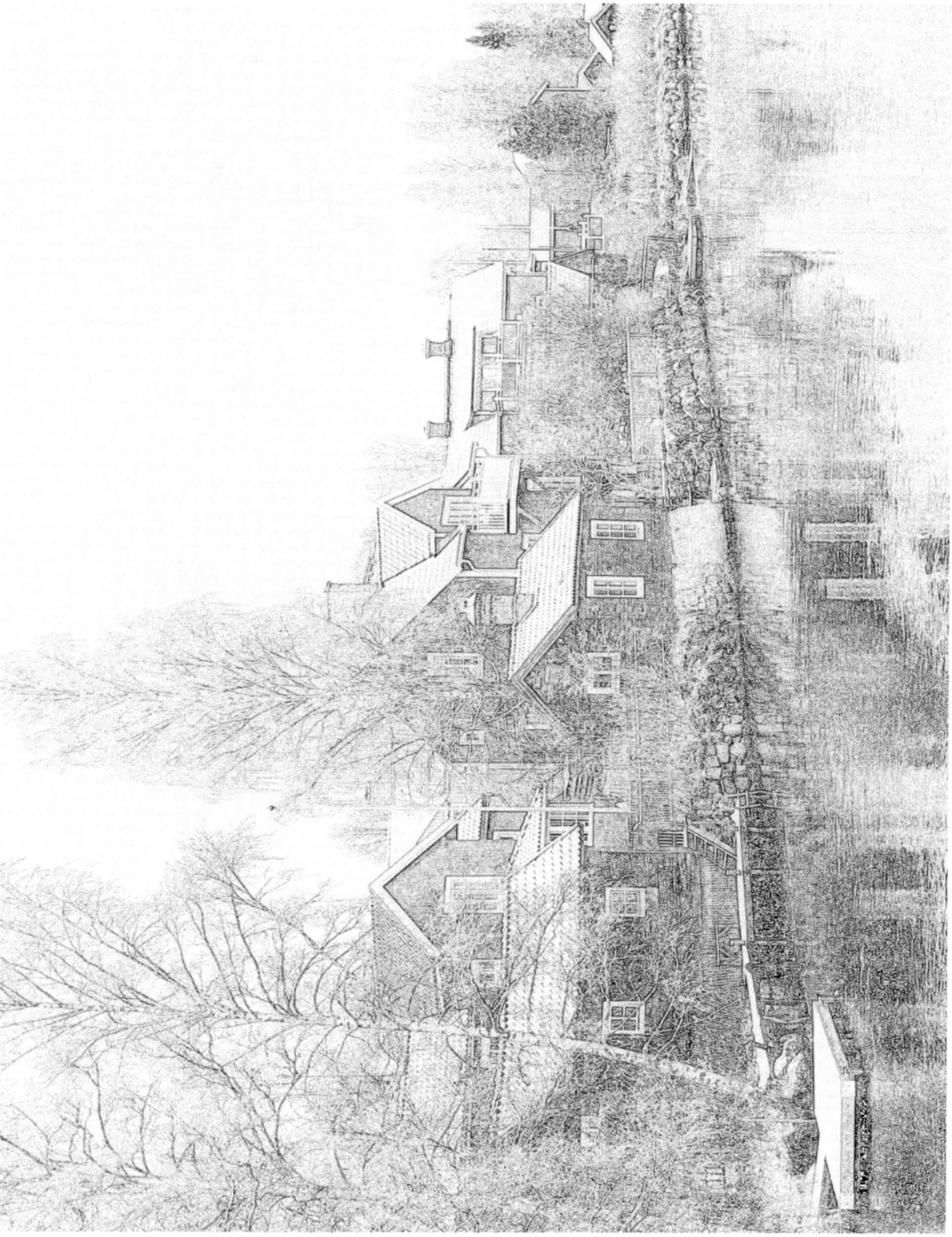

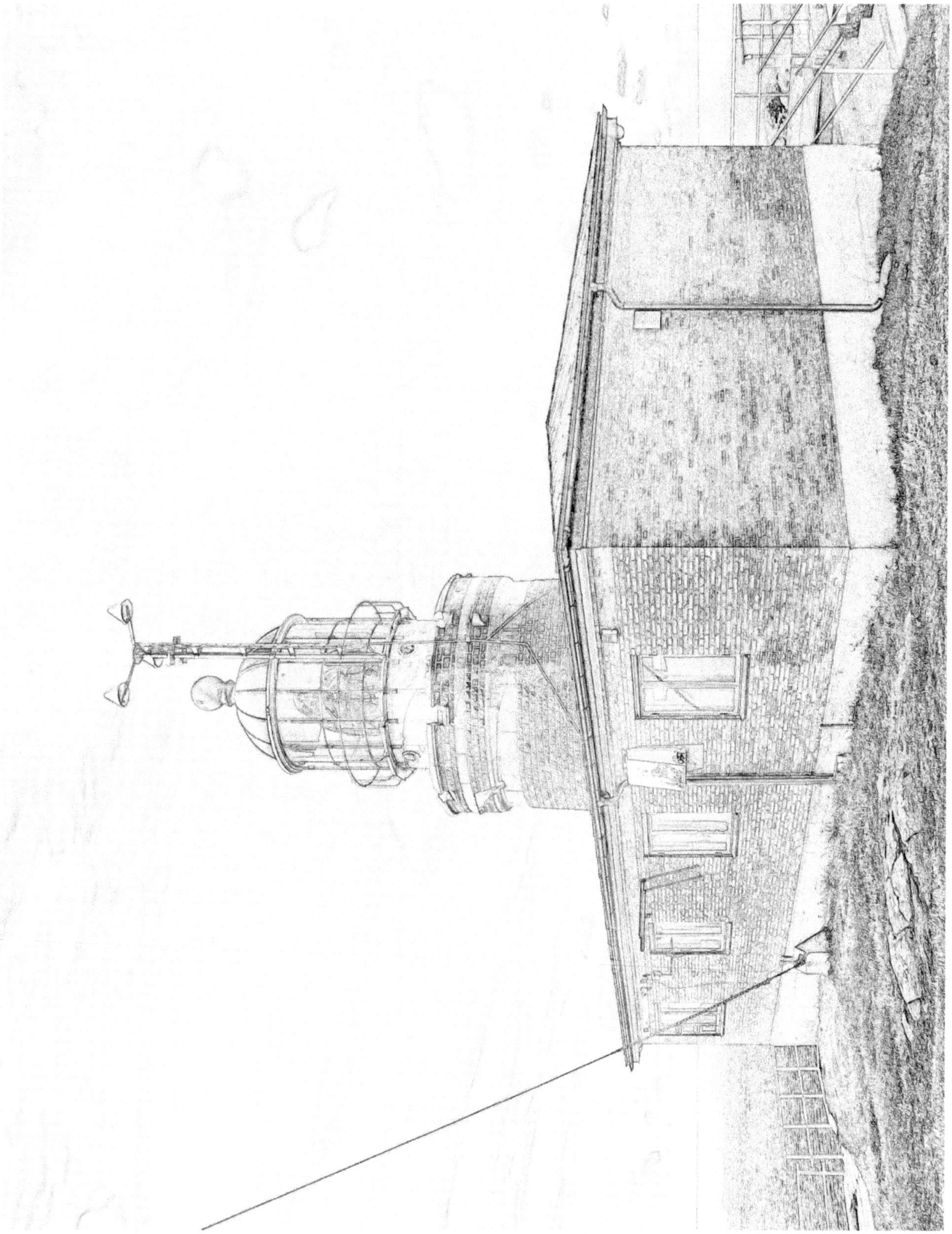

Thank you

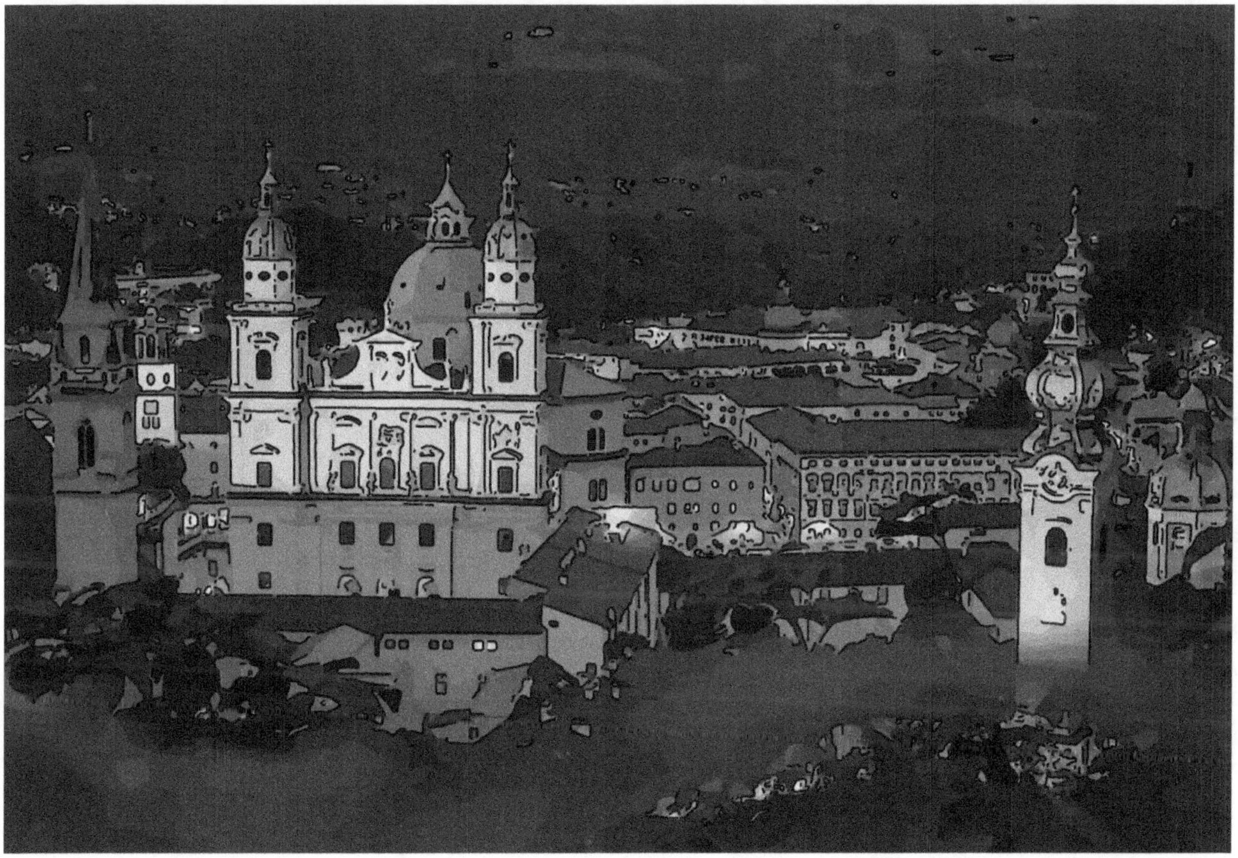

www.ingramcontent.com/pod-product-compliance
Lightning Source LLC
Chambersburg PA
CBHW080633190526
45169CB00009B/3375